# Pain in the Quiet

Poetry of Words, Thoughts, Actions, or Lack Thereof

## *Lady V Poetry*

# Pain in the Quiet

Poetry of Words, Thought, Actions, or Lack Thereof

Copyright © 2019 Lady V Poetry.

Ladyvpoetry.com

Cover Art by Shane Manier

Cover Design by Sixessful Illustraceion

ISBN 978-0-578-47651-3

# Table of Contents

LIES TO LIVE
OUT MY OWN WAY
STRINGS
SILENT DESIRE
FAILURE
QUESTION
POISON
NO TREASURE
NEW ANTHEM
GODDESS
BLACK BODIES
MORE TIME
SOCIAL MEDIA
ENVIRONMENT
BEAUTIFULLY SILENT
ORCHESTRA
YOUNG V

# Luxuries Unmissed
The luxury to be viewed as a human, before anything else

# Dedication

The inner me wants to say that this book is for me. Tell you that I put together this collection of poetry just so people would stop asking me for a book. Poetry saved the lives of many and kept me out of prison. If I am honest with myself, I would say that is correct, in part.

This collection is for anyone who has ever been told they are not good enough. The unmitigated gall to prove any naysayer wrong helped bring this collection to life. This book is for all those who gave me a word of encouragement. At the risk of leaving someone out, living or transitioned, I will not name names. You know who you are, and you are great!

To the people who get me out of my comfort zone, and demand that I go deeper with my poetry, this is for you. Thank you for the criticism and the praise. Your actions are a driving force behind the woman I am today. I look forward to what the coming years have in store for me!

**Luxuries Unmissed**

The luxury of being able to have a bad day.

# LIES TO LIVE

They say it is better to tell the truth,
the consequences are far less.
How do I respond when my answer can be the
difference in my life ending...or just continuing?

My lies never killed anyone,
but my truth will cause murder trials.
My lies can keep the lights on.
My dishonesty will keep food in my belly.
They say it is better to be honest, honest.

Yet we live in such a politically correct world
that our entire lives are lies.
Honesty is shunned like a Queen's bastard child

Lies cast out like truth trying to save the world;
Just grab on and come to this land it is safe.
They say it is better to be real, yes real.

Our recantation of reality is so fake the best
impersonators won't participate.
They see the truth and will have no parts of the
fake.

Friends telling me I'm better off just being all on
your own.

Not knowing that if I walk away from this
relationship, I will be dead.

So, I will lie
Tell you that I did not try to leave you
I only got lost on my journey home
I won't tell you that I had a full tank of gas,
and I told the GPS to take me any place, but
home because I was over all the reasons you
have for your fist meeting my back, chest, and
face.

I will hold back the truth,
telling you that I will always love you
and there is nothing that you can do about it.
I won't be honest
and tell you that my love was gone
after the 4th time you came home white boy
wasted, left no money for the electric bill
causing lies of family deaths and hospital stays
so that some charity would pay the bill.

I will be fake,
saying that I give you my heart,
and expect that I already have yours in hand
knowing damn well that you gave your heart to
no one, and the only thing left of mine
is star dust on the ground.

Lying keeps me alive,
because my man is an abusive control freak.
Dishonesty keeps food on the table
because kids can panhandle better than adults
Being fake keeps me safe
because he won't kill the lady whose world
revolves around him.

# OUT MY OWN WAY

The definition of insanity is doing the same action and expecting different results.
God wants to elevate you but no change has occurred.
No ascension to higher planes while doing the same dead work.
Time for you to get out the way-

Alone, I'd try to take flight,
Boeing.
Baggage clouding my sight,
blinded.
Holding the past had wheels chained down,
grounded.
Told God I wanted to change my life,
reborn.
His response, get out my own way.

My runway had always been clear,
crystal.
I was foolish trying to go forward- backwards,
dismal.
I desired a life where I didn't feel physical pain,
non-abusive.
Each time I tried to move I carried domestic violence inside,

broken.
My enemy was me. Blocking my own way.

My wheels couldn't go up 'cause something held me down,
relationships.
I still obligated myself to life draining people,
leeches.
Metal detector exposed the shrapnel within,
transparent.
Cavity search revealed contraband surrounding me,
breech.
The enemy continued to be me. Destroying my own way.

I let go of the issues inside of me,
inner peace.
Dissolved the rope and walls of my guarded heart,
released.
No longer tied to stagnant people,
liberty.
TSA took away everything entrapping me,
immunity.
God took control of my wheels,
piloted me.
Now I take flight to higher heights,
set free.

I am no longer in my own way.

You will have to do things you have never done, in order to obtain results, you've never seen. God wants to elevate you, but you have to get out of your own way.

# STRINGS

You,
You are puppet
Who is just sitting,
Waiting,
On its master to pick up the stick
Command action.
You had the ability to decide your own future,
Giving you release
From the strings of their control.
Instead you,
You chose to wait in limbo,
Your own man-made purgatory,
Until the time your master
Says you are worth
Their time to command.
I wish you would wake up
To know that you,
You are better than a puppet on a string.
Your life has more value
Than the master has the desire,
Capacity,
No, the ability to see.
I hope,
I hope you come
To this realization before
Everything that can be good in your life
passes you by.

You,
You are one of a kind,
A diamond in the rough,
But to get to your glory
Some mining has to be completed,
Some rocks must be broken.
The stone must be cut,
And the diamond has to be polished.
Know even,
That which is a puppet
Can be a diamond,
But first you,
You must cut
The Strings

## SILENT DESIRE

What if
I told you the woman you see
standing before you
is not the woman I see in the mirror.

What if
all the attributes your eyes behold do not
outweigh the damage imposed on my psyche
from childhood.

What if
I told you that at the age of 8 my father told me
because I was a girl there was no reason for him
to be an integral part of my life.

What If
I told you my parents were married and I was
attached to my father. I would walk on his feet to
insure our footsteps match.

What if
I told you that I felt him pry my rib cage open to
see my still beating heart.
Cut every atrium, ventricle, close all aortic
valves,
then rip my heart out of my chest

just to show me the power of his destruction.

What if
I told you at 8 years old I thought death was a better option for me because no one wanted me anyway.

What if
I told you that I had to stare my father in the eyes and ask him "am I not your child?"
"Does my life have less value than my brothers, simply because I don't have a penis?"

What if
I told you the first time I felt discrimination and the strain of a glass ceiling came from a preacher, my father, sitting on his bed before there was even the thought of a promotion, no job interview.

What If
I told you I go through life as if everyone is going to let me down.
Then, will you know why I am happy around people, but more comfortable being alone?

# FAILURE

I tried to write you a love poem.
My pen could not form the correct words.
Each time I put needle to paper,
The ink left me dissatisfied.
Oil never penetrating sheets to cause heart string motions.
Jack hammer of ball never released orgasmic greatness on white pages.
Springs lack capability to open caverns
Allowing shaft's ascension and dissension to reach climactic heights,
Like starting a journey only to stop halfway…
Disappointment.

I tried to sing you a love song
With melodies so sweet you automatically thought of me.
But with each rise and fall of vocal phrases,
I crack like lips in winter's air with no Carmex.
My notes always fall flat on the staff
Causing a sharp pain in my stomach with every crescendo and decrescendo.
My allegro was never fast enough to fill my chest with the magnitude of greatness your love brings.

I got tired of trying and failing to write you a
love poem, or sing you a love song.
Waking each morning thinking
Today will be the day I have the words to scribe
in concrete the way my heart beats for you,
Or sing to you 'til Jericho's walls fall allowing
this love to transcend this plane,
but I don't have those words.

I prayed, I prayed for the answer on how to
express my feelings.
What must I say to translate my emotions of love
and gratitude to you?
How can actions be interpreted to convey
you are my heart's realization of itself in another.
How you illuminate my darkness, just crossing
my memory.
I prayed and the answer came with the shining of
heavenly light,
piercing through dark clouds saying GOD is
love.
So simply put, I always and forever GOD you!

# QUESTION

People ask me all the time…
"Lady V why don't you have children?"
My answer is always I have a dog named
Brazen, she is 4 years old.
I'm quite content.
I love my dog don't get me wrong,
But she has the focus of a yorkie with the loyalty
of a golden retriever,
the mentality of a puppy
in a full-grown pit-bull body
that outweighs high fashion runway models.
I am a single mother to that dog,
But I refuse to be a single mother to a child.
See I live in America
Where the number of black men imprisoned
parallels the number that are killed every year.
So, the way that I look at it,
I would be just one gun shot or one traffic stop
away from planning my child's father's funeral,
Or only speaking to him at visitor's time in the
penitentiary.
So again, I say, I'm 31 and the only heir to my
legacy is a 7-year-old 120 lb. pit bull named
Brazen. I know what you are thinking…
Lady V there are more men in the world than
Black men.

To that I say you are correct and maybe you have found the nonblack one for you.
But the way my skin is set up... no,
the way my genes are set up,
the way my life is set up...any child that I have will be black.
I live in America where you being 1/16th of an oppressed race can give police the right to put a bullet in your face.
Death by cop... that is an all too common phrase.
I love people of all races,
Caucasian, Latino, Asian.
But I am a black Queen and the only man with the correct credentials to raise a child of mine will be a black King.
He is the only one who can educate my child on the daily life threats of simply sitting, walking, and driving while black.
So, until the time America changes
or I move out the country
My answer to "V why don't you have any kids?" will be "I do! I have a dog named Brazen she is 7 years old and we are quite content."

# POISON

You have a noose around your brain,
with an IV drip.
Feeding it lies,
stuffing main steam garbage to your neurons.
Don't you know that even coons
need a real meal too.
How can you survive when you gorge on the
leftovers of the media's trash?
Telling the masses to be scared of a religion.
Get away from the table,
their propaganda is rotten, you know salmonella.
When has a religion ever killed anyone? I'll wait.
But you say Isis is Muslims,
Okay the Nazi and the KKK are Christians who
killed all in the name of the Bible.
Are we placing a ban on Christians?
Last I checked we lost countless Jews and blacks
because of their attacks.
You try to write it off as a way of life then,
and we just need to forgive and forget.
I guess I'm wrong for dwelling on the past facts?
America was supposed to be the land of religious
freedom.
This new Trump era is trying to fill you with lies
saying freedom isn't for the Muslims.
The news coverage is poison.

Tell me when the hell, Muslim,
became a race or nationality.
FOX is not a credible news source.
These toxins are spilling over to the youth.
Little American Muslim girls are scared of being
deported for something that they had no part of,
no laws broken, no people killed.
They are scared to live,
when it is supposed to be free.
What has America come to?

# NO TREASURE

Your trash is not my treasure.
You are the master of disguise.
Portraying your rind peelings as star fruit trying
to satisfy my every yearn.
Your coal will never make me diamonds.
For coal to become diamonds it must endure
extreme pressure,
But you fold at the mere sight of a little work.
See, cut glass has more value than you.
The representation you gave had me thinking
your costume jewelry was one of a kind,
When in reality-
you come as plentiful as the oak tree.
That Mr. Original attitude has your Walmart
shelf life in an identity crisis.
You are a duplication of a duplicated clone of a
Rainbow outfit.
You mad 'cuz I say that you are easily replaced,
Thinking that you are my Mr. Right,
my soulmate.
God said that a man that finds a wife,
finds a good thing.
If I am the wife
don't you need to be my good thing,

and not- the bearer of my destruction?
The type of man to make paths through dense
forests for this Queen to follow with ease,
Not some simple-minded boy
to just go with the flow.
Walking through the apple orchard
like these are your fruits you sowed.
Your trash is not my treasure,
and your gold a fool would never like.
Yeah you sparkle-
Like glitter on arts and crafts
With a good gust of wind,
you fall off and bust your ass.
Expecting me to stay a permanent picture
on a dry erase board.
No honey I am a Picasso,
You are just a product of hobby lobby
in toddlers' hands,
Something only a mother could love.
You put your bullshit on a gourmet platter
and expect me to get full off of lies and deceit.
See your buffet was all you can eat,
But I rather have a home cooked
candle lit dinner just for me.
You can never make platinum encrusted
diamonds out of sand and crystals,
Even if you could it would not be worth my
sanity or my soul.
So, thank you for your time Mr. Trash collector,

This piece of art has no place in your ugly ass macaroni box.

# NEW ANTHEM

*"Home of the brave and free
Free just to murder me
Land of the beautiful
Cursed by the hate we throw
Is this the new national anthem"* (New National Anthem, TI)

This is the new national anthem

- Oh say can you see by the dawn's early light, there will be more deaths, and cause more riots. Please pray for our youth, violence has no respecter of person.
  See you all
- I pledge allegiance to the flag of the United States composed of legal killers. One nation who has forgotten about God, divided by political agenda, liberty and justice for only those who have money or right color of skin.


But hey...

- You're a grand ole flag from your back, slaves were dragged and you say for peace you stand. The emblem of the land that drug my people into a fiery grave. And my heart bleeds too from the red white and blue.

We the people in order to form a more perfect union establish justice ensure domestic tranquility. Provide for the common defense, promote general welfare, for our people and our prosperity do ordain for The United States of America.
The preamble, of which we still fall short from 1787 to today.
Think about it.
We are still 2/3rd human so we have to demand the justice we deserve.
One nation who has forgot about God will provide us with everything we need to fall hard.
We have to be the change.

# GODDESS

He called me his Athena.
The flame in his heart that kept the cold away.
His pulse beat to my metronome.
He said all of my imperfections were perfect
Right down to my crooked pinky, just like his
mother's, it's our family trait.
The epitome of greatness in this world of
sameness, too bad I didn't tell em,
I'm shy because other men had drained me dry.
I never told him that now I'm independent
I never found one I could call reliable,
Dependent, like him, allowing me to be woman,
and he take the lead role.
Gone are the joys of having things handled for
me.
I never thought it a possibility.
I am not a diva with an attitude,
I don't even like being rude,
cause he taught me better.
He is my back bone.
He knows I had a hard shell
to protect me from the pain.
My innocence smacked away at the age of 7
in the ladies room sanctuary stall.
I never told him I was silenced from telling the

truth.
One angelic Child
forced to grow up way before her time.
He loved my direct approach which I used to
keep people at arm's reach.
He was the first man I allowed in my heart
without knowing all of me.
I guess that is where I went wrong,
When he found out that his Athena had a
messed-up past, I become mortal.
I was his beauty he would shelter
from volcanic eruptions,
Not knowing I welcomed the lava because it is
better than the hell of my past.
I welcomed the fiery spews because in them I
took new shape.
I became volcanic rock.
I got reconstructed, no more am I just a shamed
molested little church girl,
his baby girl.
He wanted to be my savior,
Not knowing that on my quest for God
I met a deaconess devil in the powder room
of the fellowship hall,
telling me she should cut out my tongue,
seen and not heard.
I was no Athena just a sad little daddy's girl too
scared to continue searching for God.
But he will always be my last amen.

# BLACK BODIES

Black bodies no longer hang
Like strange fruit in only southern trees.
Black bodies are used
As target practice for militant police.
Black bodies are cast aside like trash,
Only to become hashtags
Because other black bodies
Are too scared to change outcomes.
Black bodies are stuck
In a perpetual state of insanity
Because black bodies
Keep doing the same actions
Expecting different outcomes.
The cycle is stupid.
Black body encounters scared police,
Police shoots and kills black body,
Black body becomes a hashtag
For social media,
Black body's family goes before media,
Cries for justice for slain black body.
Police goes on trial for
Killing black body.
Police found not guilty
For killing black body.
Social media is in an uproar
From lack of justice

For desecrated black body.
3 months later
Murdered black body is forgotten,
Until another black body is ripped away
On street corner
In a jail cell
On a park bench
In a gas station
In a church house
Or nightclub.
Living bodies must stop being crazy and
Break the cycle
Get off Facebook.
Hold the ones responsible accountable,
Take action
Before there are no black bodies left
To fight the lynching of
The race.

# MORE TIME

I cried today
Like really cried
I sat alone and stared at your picture
Each tear held a reason that you are loved
Each whimper a regret of words unspoken

I cried today
Like really cried
I sat lost in your smile
Captured in photograph
Hiding pain at the corners and cracks
Only if happy creases
Would have broken
The silence

I cried today
Like really cried
I sat concealed behind office walls
Overcome with emotion.
With each new picture like or status post,
My eyes swelling
Wondering if we told you
That you are loved and
Valued enough while on earth.
Now you're in a better place
And your better days

Are dawning.

I cried today
Like really cried
I sat closed from the world,
Praying time machines really exists.
Hoping that you were not gone and
I could tell you that I loved you one more time.

# SOCIAL MEDIA

Hashtag black lives matter, #AllLivesMatter
I'm tired of seeing these tags.
*Hide

I'm tired of you Facebook poets,
You twitter revolutionaries,
You Instagram rights activist.
*Hide

I'm tired of you all that know
The answer to every problem,
But never leave your computers or phones to
Bring the solution to life.
*Unfollow

When will you learn that talking about change
Will not bring change?
You must get out and take action.
*Like

I'm tired of you that see every tragedy,
Massacre, or genocide
As an opportunity to make a buck
Off of someone's pain.
*Turn off notifications

You, you are the ones that make me sick.
You are the ones that can't see
People are hurting,
You can't see people are in pain.
You only see prey that is ripe for the picking.
You are the scum that I can live without.
*Unfriend

Many have died for my right to live a free life.
I will not allow active fingers posting on
Social media to be justification
For idol hands and feet.
F*ck your Facebook group!
I will continue to get out there
To bring about the change I want in the streets.
*Share

Now pound your
Black lives matter all lives matter
Ass off my timeline.
*Logout

# ENVIRONMENT

I am a product of my environment.
A black country girl queen.
Trying to get back to the values of a time when
Martin had a dream.
You see for my generation it is not a
Dream deferred, but a dream unseen.
Too worried about gunshots and killer cops
We get no sleep.
I'm trying to get back to a time when being black
Meant you had an unlimited supply of family.
I'm talking everyone watching everybody's back.
Nowadays this crab mentality has our entire
Existence in a haze too focused on self.
Who can we turn to when we need help?
Most of the leaders just doing it for the wealth.
They don't care about the neighborhood,
Mind, body or soul.
They just want that donation because
They have another campaign to uphold.
I want to get back to the time when
Big Momma made Sunday dinner every week.
You'd sit around the kitchen table and
She'd give you wisdom to keep you on your feet.
Cause she knew that it was a cold hard world and
Those streets she didn't want you to meet.

Raised hands, non-threatening,
Raised fists for the struggle.
We must come together as a people
To correct the mindset of a nation.
Rosa sat to take a stand.
Now standing is our only option.
Release the chains of slavery
That have us in mental bondage.
God made us great people.
Be the example for the next generation.
Oppression of one, is oppression of all.
No, the war is not over, victory isn't won
But we must go on fighting until the war is done-
It's the coming of the King and
Mine ears have heard his story.
It's the coming of a King and
My eyes have seen his glory.

## BEAUTIFULLY SILENT

It's time for me to be real with you;
I have been writing erotica for years
As a means to escape-
To not look at real events that
Occurred in my life.

No one wants to hear about the real me.
They don't want to know that at the age of 7
I was the victim of so-called church folks
With their holier than thou attitude,
Of which they couldn't stand up to themselves.
I was a nice young lady
Who was wise beyond her age.
I got told that the daughter of a preacher
Should just sit and look cute
While grown folks are talking.
You have nothing to add to the conversation.
These are people who themselves-
Don't have an elementary school education.
But I was a good preacher's daughter and
I just sat there in silence,
Dreaming of better days.

No one wants to hear how at the age of 15,
I fell victim to the horrors of college life.
With the stereotypical football jocks,

Who without sports
Would not have even made it
Out of high school themselves.
Beat me within an inch of my life.
Not only leaving physical but emotional scars.
All because I valued myself worth and
Didn't want to be that female passenger
On his next train.
But you see I was a good preacher's daughter,
I remembered my only purpose
Was to sit and look cute.
So, I sat and cut in silence hoping that with each
Cut I would get closer to better days.

No one wants to hear my story.
You don't want to hear how at 22
I was the sole source of unrequited loved
From a bipolar, schizophrenic maniac.
Webster himself could not accurately define
The level of stalker he was.
You don't want to know
The amount of times I have moved
Just so the sanctity of my walls would stay pure
And no longer be violated.
I was a great preacher's daughter.
Remembering that my only purpose
Was to sit and look cute.
So, I sat in peace with my Winchester piece
Still praying for better days,

Wishing one day to know my only purpose
Was not to just sit and look cute,
But to voice my concerns on all aspects
Of my life.
I wish this day would have come
Before I took my own life.
Now I am here in this coffin
No longer sitting and looking cute,
But I have graduated to laying down...
Beautifully Silent.

# ORCHESTRA

I've watched prayers become symphonies.
Heard them serenade prime time
As if they were Philharmonic.
Black lineage shed on city streets,
The conductor queuing a melody
Revolving around red blood on black pavement.
Death of humans with darker hue as tempo.
Skin color the only common meter,
A melodic discord with no resolve.

The stage is silent.
Black mothers' solo eulogies in unison.
A chord progression on repeat.
Silent cries, of why must I bury my child,
Echoes loud as the triangle in the concert hall
Through a measure of rest.
Their questions, a call with no response.
Prayers for dying babies
Never reach the directors back,
So, the world doesn't understand
The magnitude of their loss.

I've heard the community's desire
For black blood to cause more than riots
Fall on deaf ears.
Hashtags are no longer sharp

Because they've become so natural.
Their names fall flat
Like accidental notes on the staff.
The shooter, I mean composer says
This is an isolated occurrence.
As if there is not another death,
Correction accidental note ever measures.
No need to change the key signature
If you can't recognize an issue
That needs to be addressed.
No need to change the headlines
When the next sonata will be the same.

Why didn't God show me that prayers
Aren't sharp knives to protect orchestra
From bullet's pierce?
Prayers won't crescendo
Into force field's block of early death.
The grand finale of the Orchestra
Won't reverse the loss of countless lives.
There is no way to heal a broken heart
After a child's demise
Has ripped it into a million parts.
No one told me that I love you- transposed
Means, I'll die
If you don't make it home tonight.
You never told me that I love you transposed
Means, I'll die
If you don't make it home tonight.

I'm still watching prayers become symphonies
As they serenade primetime.

# YOUNG V

Dear Baby V,
Get ready.
You are about to be taken on a gruesome ride.
Be aware of your surroundings.
Protect your mother at all cost.
Know that you will meet the devil in church,
At 7 he'll start to flirt.
He will weasel his way into your temple,
Stealing the treasure
Meant for your one true king.
Leaving behind your broken hymen,
Walls desecrated
Four years you will feel this disgrace.
Don't turn away from God,

This was not his doing.
The Devil has a way to slither
Into even the holiest actions and words.
Be strong,
Speak out
Because silence gives consent.
If you do not speak, he will never repent.
Baby V,
Know that at 12 you will feel true grief.
The loss of your only grandparent
Will send you on a downward spiral.
Know God allows us to walk

This Earth but only a short time.
Deflecting your grief
Into rage will only manifest
Into more pain and heartache.
Be strong,
Speak out
Because silence gives consent.
And you have to get ready for year 13.
This is the year that your father will tell you
That he will leave you and your mother
Because your brothers are grown and,
His job is done.
You will feel
Abandonment,
Betrayal,
Neglect,
Anger,
And discontent
All at once.
These feelings will crush your world
Like an elephant standing on a roasted nut.
You will ask him
Are you not his child?
Do you not require his guidance,
Love,
And affection.
Because you are the only girl he will stay.
Baby V,
His feeling of misery

Will translate into mental and physical abuse.
Of which the scars will never heal.
Be strong,
Speak out
Because silence gives consent,
Your physical scars may never heal.
Your mental scars will never heal.
Instead they will appear as want,
No, a need of acceptance,
From all people,
Especially the opposite sex.
Know that God can heal you.
You have no need to be accepted by man.
You are perfect
You will overcome all your obstacles.
Just be strong
Speak out,
Speak out for yourself,
Speak out for others,
Speak out for those that can't speak,
Speak out,
Because silence always gives consent.

**Luxuries Unmissed**

The luxury of removing my black skin for safety.

# About the Author

Lady V Poetry was born ReVivian Freeman, in small town South Carolina to Robert and Roslyn Freeman. From a young age she had a way with words and an ability to use them to paint pictures for any audience that allowed themselves to listen. Writing was her creative release, the place where she escaped the reality of a less progressive community who was not accepting of a girl that looked like her.

Following the death of her grandfather, William J. Frazier, Sr., Lady V Poetry found herself losing the ability to escape through the page, and it being replaced by rage and abandonment. Needing to find a new release she found poetry and took to the stage. Poetry has since been her outlet. The best form of therapy that she never knew she needed.

www.ingramcontent.com/pod-product-compliance
Lightning Source LLC
Chambersburg PA
CBHW032100150426
43194CB00006B/602